to Grace & Marlene_
from Sara & Edna
with many thanks!

BULGARIA

Viara Kandjeva
Antoniy Handjiyski

BULGARIA
KNOWN AND UNKNOWN

BORINA

Published in 2004
by Borina Publishing House

E-mail: borina@borina.com
www.borina.com

ISBN 954-500-115-1

Printed in the Czech Republic

City of Sofia: 'Banski' Square

Bulgaria is a state of thousand-year old history. She is situated on the geographic cross-road between Asia and Europe and her land was, and still is, among some of the most fiercely contested by all who have ever claimed to rule the world. Many secrets of the oldest history of mankind are hidden in her bosom. In the cave called Kozarnika, not far from the town of Belogradchik, region of Vidin, the oldest so far discovered remains of proto-humans aged 1.2 - 1.3 millions of years, were found. Two articles made of clay, which were found in Bulgarian land, with an organised system of signs on them, were considered to be the oldest proto-script in the world dated the 5th millennium BC. Six ancient mining developments in the countryside area of Mechi Kladenets (Bear's Well) traced down to a depth of 18 m and dated 4th millennium BC are reckoned to be the oldest copper mine in Europe. The earliest articles of tooled gold in Europe were found in a village knoll 'Hotnitsa' not far from the city of Veliko Tarnovo. Part of them make up compositions of rings locked with each other in such a way as to form necklaces, while most of the rest are a series of plates with heavily stylised human faces on them. Experts say these articles had some cult and ritual function and have dated them 4300 BC. In a necropolis found on the northern shore of Varna lake archaeologists found 3010 gold articles weighing a total of 6.5 kg, among which the oldest symbols of power - 2 gold sceptres - are an indisputable evidence for the emergence of the ruler's institution as early as by the end of 5th millennium BC. Apart from having here the first and richest gold and silver mines in Europe, the oldest gold mine has also been preserved until present day in Bulgarian land. It could be visited even today in the Rodopi Mountains not far from today's village of Stremtsi, region of Kardzhali. Ten or so of the entrances to the mine developments and more than 500 m of the drifts have been preserved and can be seen…

The earliest historically documented human population of Bulgarian lands was the Thracians; about them Herodotus wrote that they were "the second most numerous people after Hindus". He also mentions that 'if they were to be ruled by a single Tsar they would conquer the world'… A people that had created a brilliant civilisation that gave the world Orpheus and Spartakus… The ancient Greeks called Thracians 'thalassocrats' meaning 'the Sea Lords of the World'. One of the brightest traces they have left in the human history has come to us from the 60s of the 13th century BC, from the war of Troy: Thracian warriors, led by the legendary Tsar Rezos, fought on the side of Trojans with whom they were blood relatives. In 493 and 492 BC Thracians waged wars against the famous Persian Tsar Darius I, and in the 4th century BC against the Macedonian Tsar Phillip II the Macedon and against his son Alexander the Great (the Macedon). The ruler of the Thracians-Geti, Dromihet, managed to capture Alexander's heir Lysimachus and took him to his fortified residence Helis near today's Bulgarian town of Isperikh, region of Razgrad. Thracians bequeathed us - their direct descendants - unique gold treasures that have left the world public lost in admiration when shown in the biggest showrooms of the world; unbelievable monuments of architecture: the Kazanlak Vault and the vault near the village of Sveshtari, region of Razgrad, are on UNESCO's List of the World Cultural and Natural Heritage Sites… Between 1st and 4th century AD today's Bulgarian land was part of the Roman Empire and after its division in 395 AD remained within Byzantium as the Eastern Roman Empire was popularly known. This period also abounds with no less interesting monuments and historical events… Roman roads, buildings, vaults and tombs and the remains of more than 30 cities are a vivid proof of the Roman civilisation's high achievements in today's Bulgarian land… At that same time, between the 3rd and the 4th century AD - based on incomplete information - some 54 ethnic groups invaded these lands, subjecting what the Roman civilisation had built upon the Thracian heritage to indescribable destruction. Among all of these the Goths have been the most prominent with their presence here: the ancient city of Nove near today's Svishtov by the Danube, in the region of Veliko Tarnovo, was the residence of the Ostrogoth King Teodorikh the Great (453-526 AD), and it was in Nikopolis ad Istrum (again not far from the city of Veliko Tarnovo) where Bishop Vulfila created the Gothic alphabet in the 4th century AD, translated for the first time the Bible into the language of the Goths and thus laid the foundations of the German literary tongue. Here, in Bulgarian land the Gothic liturgical calendar was also created (and this is the oldest German calendar altogether) so it is quite correct to say that today's Bulgarian land was one of the spiritual cradles of the Old German culture. In today's Bulgarian land Alarikh I was born (376-410 AD), the Visigoth King who conquered and destroyed Rome in 410 AD thus starting the fall of the Western Roman Empire…

In 5th and 6th century Slavs settled in the Balkan Peninsula, while in the middle of the 7th century Bulgarians emerge on the scene of history: after their state formation in today's South-Russian steppe known as Great Bulgaria collapsed, one of the branches of Bulgarians led by Khan Asparukh settled in the area of the Danube delta. In an epic battle with the Eastern Roman Empire (Byzantium) Bulgarians in league with the Slavs managed to impose themselves lastingly and established a new state on these lands, Bulgaria, the only one of the European states that has preserved its original name since her beginning…

In the course of almost 600 years Bulgaria played an important role in Europe both because of its military power and because of its exceptional spiritual potential that has left remarkable traces in the European cultural and historical heritage. In her noontide during the reign of Tsar Simeon the Great (893-927 AD) and later in the reign of Tsar Ivan-Assen (1218-1241) the country bordered on three seas: the Adriatic, the Aegean and the Black… In 863 during the reign of Khan Boris I Bulgaria adopted Christianity as the official religion of the state, and the Holy Brothers Kiril and Metodiy invented the Slav alphabet. This act had far-reaching consequences - Bulgaria became the centre of the Slav Christian Orthodox civilisation… Bulgarians Christianised the whole of the Slav world between river Oder and the Ural Mountains, making a breakthrough in the Christian trilingual dogma (according to it the Christian religion was to be practised in the three holy languages only: Hebrew, Greek and Latin) and the Christianity was brought to the Slav peoples in their own language. Thus for the second time in Bulgarian land an alphabet was created and by translating the Bible and the basic liturgical books as well as the huge philosophical heritage from the antiquity into Slav language the foundations of the Slav literature were laid…

For nearly 500 years Bulgaria was under the domination of the Ottoman Empire, isolated from the development and achievements of the European peoples, and Bulgarian nation underwent a biological collapse: from 1.3 million people by the end of 15th century Bulgarian population was reduced to mere 260,000 in less than 100 years and remained so for the next two centuries… For Bulgarians under the Ottoman domination Christian religion was the only permitted manifestation of public life. This fact added to Bulgarian Christianity new public functions. Churches and monasteries were turned into islands where Bulgarian national self-consciousness was reborn and developed amidst a hostile Muslim governmental and political system.

In 18th and 19th century a movement came into existence and developed fast aiming at the restoration of the independent Bulgarian Church as well as at promoting national education and culture. As a result of heroic struggle national educational institutions were set up and in the course of a couple of decades only a network of primary and secondary schools after the latest and most progressive of the European models spread almost over all lands populated by ethnic Bulgarians; thousand of young Bulgarians continued with their higher education in the universities of Russia, France, Germany, Austria-Hungary and England. Highly educated national elite was formed, Bulgarian literature, architecture, art began developing... And so came 1870 when by a special Sultan's edict an independent Bulgarian church institution was established, the Bulgarian Exarchate. In this way Bulgarian nation was internationally recognised, and this put an end to the assimilation process and the struggle for the political liberation of the country started... In 1878 Bulgarian State was restored and the natural course of Bulgaria's national development as an inseparable part of the European Christian civilisation was resumed...

Today Bulgaria enjoys again a vivid interest in her. Re-discovered now and again she evokes admiration both with the beauty of her highly diverse nature, thousands of historical monuments narrating her ancient and rich history, and with the friendly hospitality of her fascinating people...

We believe that this brief photo-story comprising 200 colour photographs will help you preserve for life the memories of your meetings with Bulgaria and Bulgarians as well as with the roots of the European civilisation still preserved in today's Bulgarian land...

City of Sofia: A general view out to the city southern districts and Vitosha Mountain in the background

City of Sofia: the temple-monument 'Sveti Alexander Nevski' (Saint Alexander of Neva) erected in honour of the fallen in the war for the liberation of Bulgaria

City of Sofia: the monument of the Unknown Soldier in front of the south wall of the ancient church 'Sveta Sofia' (Saint Sofia)

City of Sofia: Ceremonial relief of the guard in front of the Palace of the President of Republic of Bulgaria

City of Sofia: the building of the National Assembly, erected in 1886

City of Sofia: the Council of Ministers' Building

City of Sofia: the basilica 'Sveta Sofia', 6th century AD - a general view from the east

City of Sofia: the basilica 'Sveta Sofia', 6th century AD, south facade

City of Sofia: the west gate of ancient Serdica, 4th century AD
City of Sofia: the east gate of ancient Serdica, 4th century AD

The church 'Sveti Georgi (Saint George the Victor): the best preserved antique monument in the city of Sofia

City of Sofia: ruins of the imperial complex of Emperor Constantine the Great, 4th century AD

City of Sofia: the church 'Sveti Georgi' - five layers of murals dated 10th through 14th century have been preserved

City of Sofia: the church 'Sveti Georgi' - until 1998 was a museum, today liturgies have been resumed there

A view out to Sofia University 'Sveti Kliment Ohridski' (St Clement of Ohrid) and the south-east district of the city

City of Sofia: the temple-monument 'Sveti Alexander Nevski' - east facade

City of Sofia: the temple-monument 'Sveti Alexander Nevski' - part of the west facade with the bell tower above the main entrance

City of Sofia: the crypt of the temple-monument 'Sveti Alexander Nevski' Since 1965 it has been turned into an art gallery, affiliated with the National Gallery of

Fine Art. There, unique specimens of Old-Bulgarian and Renaissance art from the period of 4th through 19th century are exhibited

City of Sofia: the People's Theatre 'Ivan Vazov', erected in 1907, west facade

City of Sofia: the building of the former hotel 'Imperial', erected 1920

City of Sofia: the building of the Chamber of Trade and Industry: detail of the north facade

City of Sofia: 'Vitosha' Blvd.- contemporary building-up of a town area

City of Sofia: Grand hotel 'Sofia', 2004 - a detail of the northwest facade

City of Sofia: the church 'Sveti Nikolay' (Saint Nicolas the Thaumaturge), erected 1912, better known as the 'Russian Church'

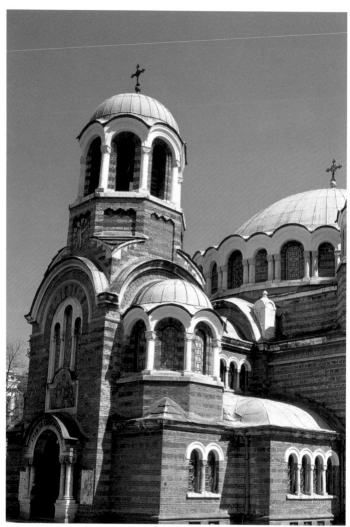

City of Sofia: the church 'Sveti Sedmochislenitsi (The Seven Saints – so the disciples of teachers Kiril and Metodiy were called), 1907; part of the southwest facade

City of Sofia: the National Palace of Culture. At the competition 'The best congress centre' for 2003 organised by the International Association of Congress Pa-

laces it was rated the second best in the world for the year 2003

City of Sofia: the Amusement Park 'Sofia Land'

City of Sofia: 23 attractions, among them a 34-m high Ferris wheel offer unfor-
gettable and exciting experiences

City of Sofia: the district of Lozenets - a general view

City of Sofia: the National Museum of History

City of Sofia: Boyana church, facade. Preserves valuable monuments of Bulgarian medieval art. On UNESCO's List of the World Cultural and Natural Heritage Sites

City of Sofia: Boyana church: portraits of the donors Kaloyan and Desislava, 1259
The life of St Nicolas the Thaumaturge: 'The miracle at sea', wall painting, 1259

Lakatnik cliffs: the most picturesque part of the Iskar Gorge.
Fifteen alpine trails are blazed along the gorge together with more than 30 caves,

the largest of which exceeds 6 km in length

Borovets, the oldest winter resort in Bulgaria. In the distance rises the snowy dome of Vitosha Mountain located to the south of the city of Sofia

Koprivshtitsa: a museum town and a reserve of architecture and history having more than 380 architectural and historical monuments

Every year the Days of Folklore are held in the town of Koprivshtitsa and once every 5 years a National Folklore Fair takes place there - an exuberant

pageant of music, songs, dances and folk costumes

Rila Monastery, founded in the 10th century AD is on UNESCO's List of the World Cultural and Natural Heritage Sites

Rila Monastery: part of the north wing and the main monastery church 'Rozhde-stvo Bogorodichno' (The Birth of the Holy Mother of God)

The main monastery church: mural decorations of the outer gallery

Rila Monastery: a medieval defence tower erected by the Protosevast Hrelyo Dragovol, 14th century

The Polsko-Skakavishki (on the river Polska Skakavitsa, a tributary to Strouma) waterfall in the Zemen Gorge of river Strouma

The earth pyramids near the village of Stob, region of Kyustendil. They were formed in yellow Old-Quaternary; a natural landmark with international importance

Town of Melnik: the smallest town in Bulgaria, a reserve of architecture and a museum town with more than 100 houses declared monuments of culture

Town of Melnik: the ruins of the so-called 'Byzantine house' built in 14th century

Town of Melnik: Pashovata kashta (the Pashov's house), mid-17th century

A village of Rozhen's house, region of Blagoevgrad

Rozhen Monastery 'Rozhdestvo Bogorodichno', founded in 1220; it has acqui-
red its contemporary outlook, the courtyard with the dwellings in particular, by

the end of 18th century

Rozhen Monastery: 'Women by the empty grave', detail, wall painting in the church's naos, 1732

'Abraham's offering': a detail from the iconostasis, carved from wood in 17th century

Rozhen Monastery: 'James' ladder', a wall painting on the church's north facade, 17th century

National Park 'Pirin': the second largest in Bulgaria, on UNESCO's List of the World Cultural and Natural Heritage Sites. The Ribnoto ezero lake, the largest

one of the Banderishki ezera (lakes) group

National Park 'Pirin': a general view out to the part of the cirque Bezbog and the Bezbog lake in winter

Town of Bansko: renaissance charm and magnificent nature; a point of departure for visits to Pirin Mountain whose majestic silhouette dominates the town

Town of Bansko: more than 150 of the town houses have been declared monuments of architecture

National Park 'Pirin': a view to the 'Strazhite' (The Guards) from the foot of the summit Todorin Vrah

Town of Bansko: the central square

Pirin Mountain: a view out to the summit of Vihren, 2915 m asl, the highest peak of the mountain and the second highest in Bulgaria

National Park 'Pirin'

The Koukers' Games are in fact a folklore theatre art expressing by the means of mimics, dances, costumes and masks, occasionally by a dialogue, certain ideas and ri-

tes of symbolic-magic meaning, blessings for good health, fertility and prosperity. They contain some elements of pre-historic pagan traditions

House next to a house, wall next to a wall, roof above the next roof: the houses in the village of Kovachevitsa, region of Blagoevgrad are the personification of the

love Bulgarians nurture for their home traditions. A reserve of architecture and history with 110 houses dated 18th-19th century preserved

The guest room with wall cupboards – the Kyorpeev's house in the town of Kotel, region of Sliven, erected 1813

The church at the Zemen Monastery: a cross-domed temple with an inscribed cross from 11th century

'Sveta Ana', an 11th century mural, in the church at Zemen Monastery
Portraits of the donors, Deyan and Doya, a 14th century mural at Zemen Monastery

City of Plovdiv: the second biggest and most important city in Bulgaria, situated picturesquely on both banks of Maritsa river and on 6 syenite hills (called 'tepe')

In the city centre of Plovdiv

In the city centre of Plovdiv

City of Plovdiv: the ancient theatre, 2nd century AD

City of Plovdiv: the ancient stadium, 2nd century AD – north section with Djouma-ya Djamiya (the Bazaar Mosque), 15th century in the background

City of Plovdiv: the ancient theatre, 2nd century AD – part of the west entrance and the scene

The domed Thracian vault near Kazanlak, 4th century BC: mural decorations. The vault is on UNESCO' List of the World Cultural and Natural Heritage Sites

National Park 'Central Balkan' (Stara Planina Mountains) over the town of Kalofer

Bachkovo Monastery 'Ouspenie Bogorodichno' (The Assumption), the second biggest after Rila Monastery and one of the oldest in Bulgaria. Founded in 1083

by the Georgian Grigory Bakouriani, Sevast and Grand Domestic of the Byzantine army

Bachkovo Monastery: part of the courtyard with the main church 'Ouspenie Bogorodichno' (The Assumption)

The church-ossuary at Bachkovo Monastery, erected in 1083. There are 11th and 14th century murals preserved in it

'Philosophers of the antiquity' and the 'Doomsday': murals from the monastery's refectory

City of Haskovo – a view out to the city park

'Sveta Bogoroditsa' (The Holy Mother of God): the 31 m tall monument in Haskovo is the tallest sculpture of Virgin Mary in the world

Town of Tryavna: a general view
Thracian shrine near Kasnakovo village, the central spring, 2nd century AD

City of Yambol: the temple 'Sveti Nikolay Choudotvorets (St Nicolas the Thau-maturge)

City of Yambol: Eski Djamiya (the Old Mosque) – an Islamic cult building erected in 1385

City of Yambol: the Thracian city of Kabile, 3rd century BC – the largest Roman military camp in the province of Thrace during 1st century AD

Mechi Kladenets: the oldest copper mine in Europe dated 4th millennium BC. Located not far from the city of Stara Zagora consisting of 6 mining developments

City of Stara Zagora: the ancient forum 'Augusta Trajana', one of most monu-
mental structures in the Roman city of Augusta Trajana (today's Stara Zagora)

preserved till present day

A picturesque meandering of river Arda, Rodopi Mountains, before its waters leave Bulgaria towards the Aegean Sea into which it flows joining first river Maritsa

The rock pyramids near the village of Zimzelen, region of Kardzhali

Perperikon: an ancient shrine that had grown into a grandiose cult centre and later in an ancient and medieval city. Inhabited without interruption since the end

of the 6th millennium – the beginning of the 5th millennium BC until as late as 14th century AD

Remains of the medieval fortress Voukelon (actually Boukelon) near the village of Matochina, region of Haskovo, in the Sakar Mountain

Agoushev's konak (the resting-place of Agoush) in Mogilitsa village. Erected in 1843, painted on the outside and inside, ceilings and cupboards made of carved wood

The Trigrad Gorge not far from Trigrad village, region of Smolyan. The cliffs on both sides of the Gorge reach 300 m in height

The precipice cave 'Dyavolsko Garlo' (the Devil's Throat) near Trigrad village. Beneath the Trigrad Gorge and down inside there are 18 underground waterfalls and lakes

The Smolyan Waterfall on river Cherna. It is located within the city of Smolyan and its water falls from a height of 21 m

The Bouynovo Gorge: the cliffs on both sides of it rise up to 350 m; at the place called 'Valchi skok' (the Wolf's leap) they are only some 10 or so metres apart

Zlatograd is the southernmost Bulgarian town of 500-year history. It is located in Rodopi Mountains amidst lovely natural surroundings, well-preserved monu-

ments of architecture and renaissance traditions, crafts and customs

The church 'Sveti Georgi Pobedonosets' (St George the Victor) and part of the reciprocal school of 1852 erected in the church's courtyard

Zlatograd sings and dances… Every year a national folk fair and singing competition named 'Rodopi Mountains and the Space' is held in the town of Zlatograd

'Dyavolski most' (the Devil's Bridge) over river Arda at the village of Dyadovtsi, region of Kardzhali. The bridge is 56 m long and 3.5 m wide and on one of the

keystones of its arch the sign of 'hexagon' can be seen

'Choudnite Mostove' (the Wondrous Bridges): three natural rock bridges up to 30 m high, the part of the river that flows under one of them is 95 m long

Rodopi's Lily (Lilium rhodopaeum), a Balkan endemic, on the Red Book of Bulgaria's List of Rare Plants

The canyon of river Vit near the village of Sadovets, region of Pleven

The Karst spring 'Glava Panega' (the head or main spring of river Panega) near Zlatna Panega village, Lovech – the second biggest Karst spring in Bulgaria

The Kroushouna travertine cascade: picturesque waterfalls, the highest one is 15 m high; located not far from Kroushouna village, region of Lovech

City of Tarnovo: a fortress and a city of Tsars, capital of the Second Bulgarian State since 1187 for 206 years, until the fall of Bulgaria under Ottoman rule

The monument of Assenevtsi (the Royal House of Assens – the liberators of the country from Byzantine yoke) in the city of Veliko Tarnovo

The church 'Sveti Dimitar Solunski' (St Dimiter of Salonika) – in it the royal princes Assen and Petar declared the uprising against the Byzantine rule in 1185

The Patriarchal temple on the hill of Tsarevets

The Patriarchal temple 'Vaznesenie Gospodne' (The Ascension of our Lord) – the interior. Modern wall paintings recreate scenes of the Bulgarian history

The church 'Sveti Petar and Pavel' (Sts Peter and Paul), erected by the end of 13th century, with three layers of paintings on its walls from 14th, 16th and

17th century – genuine masterpieces of the Bulgarian medieval painting

Nicopolis ad Istrum (the Town of Victory by the Danube) – this was what Roman Emperor Trajanus called the newly founded town to celebrate his victories over the

Dacians in 102-106 AD: preserved ruins from numerous temples with colonnades, broad streets and modern by our standards water supply & sewerage system

The church 'Rozhdestvo Hristovo' (the Birth of Christ) in Arbanasi village close to Veliko Tarnovo, the naos. Painted in stages between 15th and 17th century

The church 'Rozhdestvo Hristovo' – wall paintings in the northwest part of the gallery, 1643 AD

The Kapinovo Monastery 'Sveti Nikola' not far from the village of Kapinovo, founded in 1272, part of Tarnovo's Sveta Gora (Holy Mount)

City of Rousse: the Dohodno Zdanie building erected in 1902

City of Rousse: the elegant facades of the buildings are decorated with colonnades, sculptures, masks, devices and other details

In their running north, towards the Danube, the waters of river Cherni Lom form picturesque meanders near the village of Cherven, region of Rousse; ancient for-

tresses were erected on the hills rising between meanders. On one of these hills the fortress Cherven (12th – 14th century) stood

Ivanovo Rock Monastery, 13th – 14th century, not far from Ivanovo village, Rousse region. It was built with the funds and support provided by Tsar Ivan-Assen II

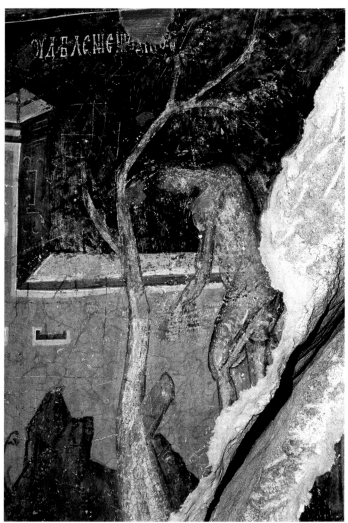

(1218-1241). 7 rock churches and chattels decorated with wall paintings. On UNESCO's List of the World Cultural and Natural Heritage Sites

City of Lovech: first a Thracian settlement, then a Roman road station Melta, it played an important role in the Middle Ages when was called Lovats. In 1187, after an

unsuccessful 3 months siege the Eastern Roman Empire was forced to sign the peace treaty thus formally recognising the restoration of Bulgarian State

City of Lovech: a general view. In the foreground is the district of Varosha – a reserve of architecture and history

The only covered bridge in Bulgaria is in Lovech. It was built by master-builder Kolyo Ficheto in 1872-1874

Town of Troyan's Monastery 'Ouspenie Bogorodichno' (The Assumption) is a functioning, male, stavropygial (i.e. subordinate directly to the Holy Synod) monastery,

the third largest in Bulgaria after Rila and Bachkovo monasteries. Annals dated 1835 tell that it was founded in 1600 by the abbot Kalist

The cliff on which the Màdara Horseman was hewn in living rock. In 12th-13th century more than 170 monastic cells and rock churches were hewn in the cliffs, while

on the plateau above stood the Bulgarian fortress Màtora. Today the area of Màdara is declared a reserve of history and archaeology

The Màdara Horseman: a bas-relief hewn in living rock at a height of 23 m on cliffs near Màdara village in 8th century. On UNESCO's List of the World Heritage Sites

Màdara is the most important cult centre of the Bulgarian State before the adoption of Christianity as an official religion

Pliska: the first capital city of Bulgaria from the time the state was founded till 893 AD

Veliki Preslav: it was the second capital city of Bulgaria (from 893 till 972); remains of Tsar Simeon's palace

City of Razgrad: The clock tower (1764) mentioned by the Danish engineer Karsten Nibour who visited th city in 1767

Among the noteworthy sights in Razgrad is the mosque of Ibrahim Pasha erected in 1614. It is the second biggest mosque in Bulgaria

The ethnographic complex in the district Varosha of the city of Razgrad: presents the most attractive and typical scenes of the way of life, the ideas, beliefs and the

system of customs and traditions of the ethnic group of Kapantsi – direct descendants of the Proto-Bulgarian ethnic group

Thracian vault under the Ginina knoll not far from the village of Sveshtari, region of Razgrad, 3rd century BC. The central chamber of the vault is decorated with

caryatids – sculptured female figures. On UNESCO's List of the World Cultural and Natural Heritage Sites

An epitaph in a rock church near Krepcha village, 10th century
Rock monasteries in the valley of Souha Reka river

The rock monastery "Sveti Dimitar Basarbovski': the only functioning rock monastery in Bulgaria

A vault of the late antiquity not far from the city of Silistra, 4th century AD

Part of the medieval fortified wall of the fortress Drastar (today's city of Silistra)
Lake Srebarna, on UNESCO's List of the World Cultural and Natural Heritage Sites

Rock paintings in the cave Magourata by the village of Rabisha, region of Vidin:
Bronze Age. Paintings were made with bats' guano and depict humans and

animals performing cult rites

The Great Stalactone, a calcite formation in the cave Magourata; it is 20 m high and 4 m thick at the base

'Oknata' (Windows): openings in the arch of the cave 'Prohodna' near Karloukovo village. During the Neolithic period the cave's entrance was inhabited by man

The 'Belogradchik Rocks': a gigantean rock world that strikes imagination with wondrous shapes sculptured by the elements. Spread on a strip of land 30 km

long and 5 km wide; by one of the groups there is a fortress erected as early as in the 3rd-4th century AD and used until the 19th century

The medieval fortress 'Baba Vida' close by the Danube city of Vidin. It has been built as early as in the 3rd century and has been in use until 19th century

'Stambolkapiya', 18th century: part of the city of Vidin's system of fortifications
City of Vidin: the library of Osman Pazavntoglu, 1800

Part of the Vratsa divide of Stara Planina Mountains near the village of Zgori-grad, region of Vratsa

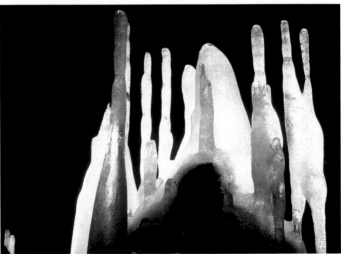

The cave 'Ledenika' not far from the city of Vratsa: the Concert Hall
Ice formations in the cave 'Ledenika'

A picturesque road goes to the very crest of the Vratsa Ridge of Stara Planina Mountains not far from the city of Vratsa

Vratsa: the residential and defence tower of Kourt Pasha's family, 17th century

The Glozhene Monastery
Town of Byala: a 14 arches bridge built by the master-builder Kolyo Ficheto in 1867

City of Sliven: a general view out to the city
City of Sliven: the church 'Sveta Sofia – Premadrost Bozhiya'

City of Sliven: part of the facade of a house from 19th century

City of Varna: the Drama Theatre building erected in 1856

City of Varna: the seaside park
City of Varna: the Roman Thermae, 2nd century

City of Varna: the cathedral 'Ouspenie Bogorodichno' (The Assumption). The temple was erected in honour of the fallen in the Russian Turkish war of 1877-1878 for

the Liberation of Bulgaria. The first sod was turned by the first Bulgarian Prince after the Liberation, Alexander Batemberg, on August 22, 1880

Town of Nesebar: a general view; on UNESCO's List of the World Cultural and Natural Heritage Sites

Town of Nesebar: the church 'Pantocrator' (God Almighty), 14th century, one of the 41 medieval churches that have been preserved till present day

The seaside resort complex 'Slanchev Bryag' (Sunny Beach) not far from Nesebar

The seaside resort complex 'Slanchev Bryag' has one of the best beaches on Bulgarian Black Sea coast

Nesebar: a narrow isthmus connects the old and new districts of the town
Seaside resort complex 'Sveti Vlas': a general view out to it from Nesebar

Ancient vault-mausoleum near the town of Pomories, region of Bourgas, 3rd-4th century AD

Rock complexes in the area called 'Yaylata' by the Kamen Bryag village, region of Dobrich used for more than 2500 years as shrines, dwellings and churches

City of Bourgas: the central railway station

City of Bourgas: the central part of the town
City of Bourgas: a general view

Town of Sozopol: the fishermen's boat jetty

Town of Sozopol: the old town

Town of Sozopol: more than 100 houses in the old town dated 18th and 19th century have been preserved as monuments of architecture

Town of Sozopol: a souvenir shop

Town of Sozopol: an architectural ensemble in the old town
Town of Sozopol: one of the five town beaches

The Biosphere Reserve 'Kamchiya': here some of the most representative riverine forests in Europe have been preserved in the area around the river Kamchiya's

mouth. The reserve was included in the international programme 'Man and the Biosphere'

National Park 'Rila': covers 30% of Rila Mountain and is the largest national park in Bulgaria with a total surface area of 81046 ha; more than 100 peaks rise within

the park boundaries, the altitude of every one exceeding 2000 m asl including the summit Moussalla at 2925 m asl – the highest point in the Balkan Peninsula

The mouth of river Veleka: protected area with international importance; located north of Sinemorets village, region of Bourgas. The protected area covers the mouth

of the river proper whose waters, when stopped by a sandbar - overflow and flood
the area on both sides of the river at a distance of over 50 m

BULGARIA
KNOWN AND UNKNOWN

with 200 colour illustrations

Text and photos: Viara Kandjeva, Antoniy Handjiyski
Graphic design: Antoniy Handjiyski
English translation: Vladimir Pomakov
Prepress: Geo Kovatchev

BORINA Publishing House
E-mail: borina@borina.com
www.borina.com

ISBN 954-500-115-1

Printed in the Czech Republic